ECHO ECHO

CARDIFF
YESTERDAY
Book Five

ᵛ

(*Overleaf*) This view was taken from the Castle clock tower *c*.1871 and shows in the middle foreground the narrow Castle Street and Angel Street divided by a block of buildings (see 67) which was demolished in 1878. Prominent in High Street is the National Provincial Bank (now Laura Ashley), while to the right of St John's Church is Zion Calvinistic Methodist Chapel which was replaced by the first part of the Central Library in 1882

STEWART WILLIAMS'

CARDIFF YESTERDAY

Book Five

FOREWORD BY
GEOFF DART

BARRY

First published September, 1982

© Stewart Williams, Publishers,
Barry, South Glamorgan

ISBN 0 900807 52 0

ACKNOWLEDGEMENTS

Grateful thanks are extended to the following for giving us permission to reproduce their photographs:

John F. Andrews (79); S. Bourge (212); D. G. Bowen (176, 180); John Bowler (111); Ron Brabyn (89, 90, 91, 92, 93, 94, 95, 98, 99, 104); Cardiff Central Library (1, 2, 3, 4, 5, 6, 9, 10, 11, 12, 13, 25, 26, 27, 28, 31, 32, 33, 34, 49, 50, 62, 67, 68, 77, 108, 134, 144, 145, 146, 147, 148, 153, 167, 169, 195, 196, 197, 198, 199, 200, 201, 203, 205); Colin Champion (216); Mrs Millicent Collard (83, 84, 85, 86); *Commercial Motor* (177, 178); Mrs Rita Davies (65); Albert Donovan (96, 97); W. E. A. Dunn (118, 124, 126, 127, 128, 129); A. G. Edwards (55, 56, 57, 58, 59); Phil Edwards (100, 101, 102, 103); Mrs A. M. Ellis (41); Fred Evans (87, 88); Lionel V. Evans (80); Bob Frank (121); R. Griffin (211); Reg Hoskins (137, 138, 139); Ray Jenkins (112, 113, 120); Miss Barbara Jones (29, 42, 43, 45, 75, 76, 132, 162, 193, 194, 213); Fred Jones (15, 16, 17, 18, 19, 20, 21, 30, 35, 39, 40, 52, 64, 66, 69, 70, 71, 72, 78, 109, 116, 133, 149, 151, 152, 159, 160, 161, 170, 171, 172, 173, 186, 190, 202, 206, 207, 208); Mr and Mrs Jack Julian (140, 141, 142, 174, 214); P. J. Kellaway (130, 131); Herbert Langlois (81, 82, 110, 163, 164); A. Maidment (74); S. Mansfield (36); E. & N. Matthews (51); James R. McIntyre (117, 150, 154, 158); Mrs. L. M. Mortimer (114, 209, 210, 215); C. Nicholls (106, 107, 155); Terry O'Connell (105); E. D. Paines (156, 157); Mrs W. M. Parry (37, 38, 44, 165, 166); Nicky Payne (143); Mrs M. Paynter (125, 192, 204); *Picture Post* (48); H. B. Priestley (181, 182, 183, 184, 185, 187, 188, 189); Billy Rees (136); Mrs Audrey Sawchuck (122, 123); L. E. Steele (168); Chris J. Taylor (175, 179); Welsh Folk Museum (7, 8, 14, 22, 23, 24, 63, 73, 115, 119, 135); S. Whittle (191); Wiggins Teape Ltd. (61); Arthur Williams (53, 54); S. Williams (46, 47, 60)

Printed in Wales by D. Brown & Sons Ltd., Cowbridge and Bridgend, Glamorgan

Foreword

by GEOFF DART
South Glamorgan County Librarian

This is the fifth *Cardiff Yesterday* book which 'Williams the Books' has produced in two and a half years. In itself this is a remarkable achievement but it is also a worthy example of Cardiff's long tradition of recording local history through the camera lens.

In September 1891, my great innovating predecessor, Mr (later Sir) John Ballinger, read a paper at the Annual General Meeting of the Library Association entitled 'Free Libraries and the Photographic Survey of Counties'. He described the scheme initiated in the previous year whereby members of the Cardiff Photographic Society would make a photographic record of Glamorgan for the Library; in return the Free Libraries Committee would award gold, silver and bronze medals for the three best collections. The Committee was of the opinion, since proved to be fully justified, that the Library would thereby 'have a unique record of the present state of the district which will be invaluable in time to come'. Other districts were not slow to follow Cardiff's example and transatlantic interest was aroused. Thirty-two framed examples of this pioneer Survey, no doubt including some of the Collings views reproduced in this book, were displayed as part of the Library Association's exhibit in Chicago during the World's Fair of 1893.

The *Shell Book of Firsts* confirms that Cardiff was again the venue of photographic pioneering in 1896, this time in the field of moving pictures. On 27 June the Prince and Princess of Wales (later King Edward VII and Queen Alexandra), with their daughters Princesses Maud and Victoria, arrived in Cardiff to visit the great Cathays Park Exhibition and to open the completed Central Library. The visit coincided with the presence in the town of Birt Acres who had been demonstrating his 'Kineopticon' invention to the Photographic Society. A local consulting engineer and member of the Society, S. W. Allen, tells us in his delightful book of reminiscences how he and Acres were permitted to film the arrival of the Royal Party at the Exhibition through a peephole in a canvas screen. By command of the Prince, the film was exhibited by Acres before an international array of royal guests on the eve of the wedding of Princess Maud (subsequently Queen of Norway) a month later. This was the first newsfilm of a non-sporting event made in Great Britain and the first Royal Command Film Performance. If not the first, it was almost certainly one of the first such films to be exhibited commercially, because it was shown several times daily in the replica of the old High Street Town Hall at the Cardiff Exhibition, the price of admission being six (old) pence.

No copy of this seminal newsfilm is known to have survived, but the work of the thirteen principal contributors to the 1890 Survey to-day constitutes one of the fundamental elements of the Central Library local collection. Now, almost a century later, Stewart Williams is promoting another major project in the field of both written and visual Cardiff history, but with one crucial difference. Whereas the participants in the first Survey formed a small group, nearly all amateurs, who were leisured and affluent enough to pursue their expensive hobby, the contributors to *Cardiff Yesterday* are numerous and widely spread, with each new volume encouraging more potential participants to seek out family albums and to search the recesses of bureaux.

Not all the contributors to *Cardiff Yesterday* No. 5 are contemporary, however; most of the photographs of the 1868-95 period were taken by a remarkable professional 'photographic artist' and his family. He was Joseph Collings of Bute Street, a watchmaker by trade, who seems to have perceived very early on that the camera could record permanently the impermanent. Sadly he died prematurely about 1875 but his widow Margaret and later his sons carried on the business and seem to have inherited his perception; this can be deduced from a typical example. The graceful forty-year-old Gas, Light and Coke Co. Offices in Bute Terrace captured for posterity in 1895 in the nick of time—the demolition men have already removed one window frame! Other favourites of mine are St Peter's Church, Roath, about 1870 before its final completion to the plans of Charles Hansom, brother of Joseph the cab designer; that supreme example of money being no object, the sumptuous temporary ballroom etc. built in the Castle environs for a 'one night stand' to celebrate the Coming-of-Age of the Marquess in 1868; and the huge scaffolding erected by Richard Greaves for the building of the Castle Clock Tower, drawing on his experience of twenty years before when the towering columns of Stephenson's Britannia Bridge were being constructed.

Could any old (and not so old) citizen turn the pages of this book without encountering scenes which trigger off a whole train of memories? Surely I am not exceptional in this. I have already mentioned the beautiful St Peter's Church, in whose shadow I was reared and to whose 'elementary' school and its dedicated teachers I owe so much. There is the *Tavistock Hotel*, known locally as 'The Tavvy', whose all-male outing group portrayed in the 1925 photograph had a ladies' counterpart entitled (unless memory is being a fickle jade) 'The Tavistock Tidy Women's Club'. These two photographs recall in turn the bustling City Road of the twenties, before it was invaded by the devotees of the great god CAR (whose most impressive temples seem now to have been taken over by newer gods CARPET and BOOZE). John Williams, our grocer's shop on the corner of Milton Street, a family concern in all senses of the word, with Billy Featherstone presiding over the massive bacon-cutter and never at a loss for a bantering word with even the most staid customer. Gus Corke's 'all kinds of everything' shop, an Aladdin's cave which distracted us on our way to the Saturday afternoon 'tuppenny rush' at the Gaiety (now a temple of the god BINGO). I am surprised to find that Gus is described in contemporary directories only as a 'bird dealer and corn merchant'. My adolescence in the 1930s is recalled by the photographs of Jack Peterson's meteoric career, particularly a day in December 1932 when that gentleman giant, heavyweight champion of Great Britain, could find time to return to St Illtyd's, where he had been a pupil not many years before, and visit individually every classroom. With Max Boyce, albeit in a different sporting context, I can say 'I was there'—in Form IV. One is tempted to go on ad infinitum or, at least, ad nauseam.

I am grateful to Stewart for giving me the opportunity to assist with the exact identification and dating of some of the puzzles which the books engender in process of compilation. This is a fascinating task in its own right, but to a librarian the greatest satisfaction is the new information which comes to light and which creates new pieces for the jigsaw of Cardiff's local history. I can never achieve full native status in the terms of Frank Hennessy's ballad because I am not Cardiff-born (that dubious honour belongs to Neath). Perhaps, as with one of the qualifications for claiming hereditary freemanship, I could claim honorary native status, having had a Cardiff-born father-in-law whose daughter is herself no mean contributor to Cardiff's Victorian history with fact and fiction. As a last resort, I could achieve posthumous status by virtue of Frank's secondary qualification 'when I dies, I'll be Cardiff dead'. I am in no hurry to qualify for the last-named; I might miss Cardiff Yesterday No. 6 and its successors.

Geoff Dart

AUTHOR'S NOTE

This latest book in the *Cardiff Yesterday* series is rather special so far as I am concerned because it features my boyhood idol Jack Peterson whose famous exploits in the ring have brought great credit to the sport and to his native city. For providing these and other splendid boxing photographs I am grateful to Ron Brabyn, himself no mean amateur boxer in the 1930s.

Once again I am pleased to acknowledge my indebtedness to the many kind people who have provided me with photographs. They are listed elsewhere, but I must express special thanks to Cardiff Central Library, the Welsh Folk Museum, Miss Barbara Jones, Fred Jones, Bill Barrett, Derrick Jenkins, Chris Taylor, Dennis and Bill O'Neill who went out of their way to help.

The splendid foreword is the work of my friend Geoff Dart, County Librarian of South Glamorgan, whose encylopaedic knowledge of the city has already added so much to the series, while the end-paper drawings are by 'Gren' the *South Wales Echo* cartoonist whose subtle humour and unique style have made him one of the best in the country.

Thanks to the keen interest taken right from the start in *Cardiff Yesterday* by Geoff Rich, editor of the *South Wales Echo*, whose knowledge and love of the city are well-known, the series has reached a wide and receptive audience in South Wales and beyond. CBC and Frank Hennessy in particular have also given valuable coverage to the books. I continue to be extremely grateful.

STEWART WILLIAMS

City, Suburbs and Docks

2 Cardiff Castle clock tower and (*right*) *Cardiff Arms Inn*, c.1876. The tower was completed in 1872 and three years later the Third Marquess of Bute began growing vines against the castle wall. The inn was demolished in late 1882

3 St Mary Street, *c.*1882. Guildhall Place was opened following the demolition of the old Town Hall (*centre, left*) in 1913-14

4 These old shops were situated near the Castle Arcade in High Street, *c.*1874. On the extreme right is part of the Brecon Old Bank (now Lloyd's)

5 This was the approach to the Castle from High Street in 1876. High Corner House and the adjacent buildings were removed to improve the approach soon after this was taken

6 View from Castle clock tower looking west, *c*.1871. On the left, Mark Street, Coldstream Terrace and Brook Street are under construction on land owned by General Sir *Mark* Wood of the *Coldstream* Guards. In the middle distance (*right*) trees show the line where the lower (or terraced) portion of Cathedral Road was later built

7 Open-air market stalls outside the Central Library in the Hayes, 1898. In June 1892 street
   hawkers were permitted to sell goods on this open space subject to a toll of 6d per truck

8 Duke Street from the east, *c.*1912, with the *Law Courts Hotel* on Kingsway corner (*right*).
   Duke Street was widened in 1923

9 This property on the corner of Church Street and St Mary Street was originally the family residence of 'Squire' William Richards, a well-known Cardiff landowner. It was occupied by Edwin Dobbin, stationer, when this was taken in 1903

10 On the top of this massive wooden structure was a travelling gantry which lifted the stones—some of them weighing five tons—to make the Castle clock tower, designed by William Burges and completed in 1872

11   Cardiff Castle *c*.1866, before the left hand wing was demolished by the Third Marquess of
Bute to make way for the existing guest wing and tower

12   Entrance to Cardiff Castle, *c*.1870

13 Custom House and old *Custom House Hotel*, c.1875. The hotel was demolished for the widening of Custom House Street and cutting of New Street c.1878. The Glamorganshire Canal is in the foreground

14 Old premises adjoining St John's Schools in Queen Street. Schools and shops were demolished in 1912 to make way for Principality Buildings and Priory Street (renamed The Friary in 1925 for the sake of monastic accuracy)

15 Clive Street, Grangetown, in 1908

16   Merthyr Road, Whitchurch, in 1910

17   Mrs Florence Mazdon's Old Oak Restaurant which stood near the corner of Pantmawr Road, Whitchurch. Judging from the newspaper placards it was taken during the First World War

18/19 These early views of Ty-glas Road and (*below*) Station Road, Llanishen, reflect the leisurely pace of early twentieth-century life before the motor car made its impact on the environment

20 Whitchurch Road before the extension tram tracks to North Road were opened in June 1928

21 A semi-rural looking Pantbach Road in the 1920s

22/23/24 Life could be hard in the backstreets of Victorian Cardiff. Mary Ann Street (*opposite and centre*), ran from Bute Terrace to Bridge Street

The faces reflect hope and despair in equal measure. Sanitation was poor, money short and luxuries non-existent. The year was 1893

In the suburbs, too, many were caught in what we now call 'the poverty trap'. These youngsters in Halket Street (renamed Avon Street in 1910), Canton, were facing a depressing future in 1892

25/26 Time had not touched the rural tranquillity of Leckwith village when these views were taken in the early years of this century. Inevitably road improvements and housing development have since swept away much of this 'chocolate box' image

27/28 What still remains recognisable, despite road widening and a new viaduct (opened in 1934), is Leckwith hill whose steep gradient has always been difficult to negotiate. The old stone bridge has been preserved and is a listed building

29 Swiss Cottage, Fairwater, with a hayrick in the garden, *c.*1914. This attractive building, with its 'barley stick' chimneys, was demolished in February 1972

30 Brachdy Road, Rumney, *c.*1917

31 Entrance to Roath Basin, early 1874. The Basin was opened on 23 July 1874

32 Bute Warehouse, Bute East Dock, c.1871. This listed iron-framed building (a very early example) was built in 1861 to the designs of the engineer, W. S. Clark

33 Clarence swing bridge under construction, May 1889. It was opened by the Duke of Clarence and Avondale in September 1890 and replaced by a new static bridge opened by the then Prime Minister, James Callaghan, MP, on 9 April 1977

34 This low water pier was opened in 1868 but proved unsuccessful and was truncated in the mid-1890s when this was taken

Trade and Industry

35 J. F. Grainger's well-stocked shop in 7/8 Working Street (near the Queen Street Arcade entrance), 1907. The shop continued to trade until the 1930s. Grainger had a rope works in Roath

36 Enos Needs, fruit and vegetable salesman of Flora Street, Cathays, poses with his prize-winning pony and cart outside Minny Street Welsh Baptist Church, c.1898

37/38 The Park Newsagency, 109 Albany Road, on the corner with Wellfield Road, December 1901. It was demolished along with the adjoining property in *c*.1913-14 for the construction of the Penylan (now Globe) cinema. The owner was the son of D. Davies (*below*) who ran his boot and shoe repairing depot in Albany Buildings, Wellfield Road (to the side of the Globe) in 1903

39 A traffic-deserted Cowbridge Road, Canton, in 1910. A. D. Davis the fruiterer (*left*) was sited in the block between Turner Road and Lionel Road

40 In 1915 S. Edelman's Cathedral Art Studios were also in Cowbridge Road, Canton, near the City Lodge (now St David's Hospital). Edelman was the father of the late Maurice Edelman, novelist and MP for Coventry

41 Down the years the corner shop has provided a valuable service to local communities. Seventy years ago this one on the corner of Robert Street and Gower Street, Cathays, like many others in various parts of the city, stocked much more than groceries, was open all hours, and evidently believed in the power of advertising!

42 Bon Marché on the corner of Woodville Road and Crwys Road, c.1912

43 In 1908 Bon Marché had two shops in Woodville Road, a drapers and milliners on the left hand corner, and a furniture shop on the right near the May Street intersection

44 These charming young ladies worked for the Domestic Bazaar Company, 72 Queen Street, in 1907. The donor's mother, Miss Emma Olive Lewis (*front right*) became under manageress before leaving to get married

45 Co-op shirt factory on the corner of Bute Terrace and Mary Ann Street taken in the mid-1920s before automation

46/47 Spillers Nephews biscuit factory (now Leo's) was established in Moorland Road in 1896. Here Albatross flour was prepared and about 5,000 boxes of biscuits packed and despatched daily. (*Above*) the export packing room, and (*below*) the large bakery

48 Cardiff's first 'Lord Sandwich' and one of its most colourful characters in the 1930s and 40s was 'Colonel' Charles Jarvis who, immaculately attired in top hat, brolly and spats, paced the city streets advertising, at various times, Harrison's second-hand clothes shop in Albany Road and the Embassy Skating Rink in Cathays Terrace. Some will remember him dressed as a Romany advertising Waldini's Gypsy Band at Roath Park Pavilion

49 The Carlton in Queen Street offered 'unlimited bakestones, French or brown bread and butter and jam' for 8d in the 1920s and this to the accompaniment of an orchestra. For the sports-minded there were 22 billiard tables. Owned by R. E. Jones it remained for many years a popular rendezvous with Cardiffians of all ages

50 The *Borough Arms* (renamed the *Bodega c.*1897) was dwarfed when Solomon Andrews erected his Market Buildings in 1886. Owned then by James Howell, the draper, it has always been one of the most popular pubs in St Mary Street. It reverted to its original name in 1961

51   Staff (including the errand boy with bicycle clip) outside the Argyll Stores on the corner of Albany Road and City Road, 1937. The Quartermaster Stores now occupies the premises

52   A Government rehabilitation scheme for discharged soldiers in 1918 when tailoring offered a worthwhile future

53 Coal carts were a common sight in the 1920s and 30s. F. J. Williams & Sons of North Church Street had just taken delivery of these in the late 1920s

54 Cardiff coal merchants' outing c.1930

55/56 Alfred George Edwards (*left*) started his bakery business on the corner of Evelyn Street and Adelaide Place in 1911. He continued to trade from the Docks until 1924 when the Edwards family opened their Garden City Bakery in Ely (*below*). The business prospered under the founder's capable direction and at one time, in addition to the bakery which served most of Cardiff and outlying townships, Edwards's owned 11 shops and three cafes

57 With this stallion 'Rumney Viscount' A. G. Edwards bred his own horses for use in the business

58 The bread roundsman's horse-drawn van was a commonplace sight in the 1920s and 30s

59 A. G. Edwards died in 1932 and the business was taken over by Thomas & Evans. Alfred George (Junior), *right*, who worked alongside his father in building up Edwards's, opened his own bakery in 1936 but was forced to close two years later due to ill health

CROSS BROS.
Ltd.

"The Cardiff Ironmongers"

---

3 & 4, ST. MARY STREET.

Deliveries Free by Rail on purchases of £2 to all parts of the Kingdom.

Bedsteads.

Bedding.

SILVER.

Electro-Plate.

Cutlery.

GARDEN FURNITURE

TOOLS.

At Our Well-known

Low Prices.

Deliveries Twice Daily to all parts of the City.

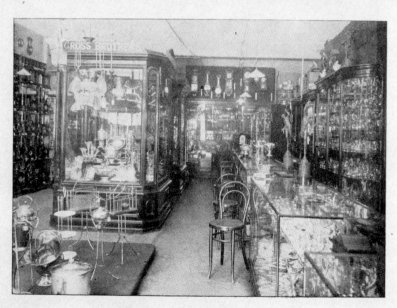

A corner of the Electro-plate and Silver Department.

Cross Bros., Ltd., the Well-known House for Wedding, Birthday and other Presents.

60 Cross Brothers' department store was a feature of St Mary Street from the 1880s until 1935 when a fire destroyed the premises. They also had an ironmongery business in Working Street for many years

61 Brown and Evans' Ely Paper Works (later Thomas Owen's and now Wiggins Teape Ltd), 1865

62 Cardiff Gas Light and Coke Company's offices in Bute Terrace, demolished in 1895. In 1901 there were 15,500 consumers and 2,911 public lamps. The price charged was 3s 4d per 1,000 cubic feet

63　Hancock's dray arriving with supplies of beer for Lock's of Broadway, Roath, in 1906

64　Ely has a long association with malting and for many years the two breweries—Ely and Crosswells—were prominent landmarks from the bridge. The former claimed special qualities for its ales by virtue of the water drawn from its artesian well

65 The *Glendower* on the corner of Crichton Street and East Canal Wharf, *c*.1910

66 An advertisement card for the *Tresillian* in Tresillian Terrace, *c*.1912. It was destroyed by enemy action in the Second World War

67 *Cowbridge Arms*, Broad Street, *c.*1870. This block of buildings was removed in 1878 enabling Angel Street and Castle Street to be merged

68 *Royal Hotel*, St Mary Street, *c.*1870. The properties on the left and the house on the right have since been added to the hotel

TELEPHONE
No. 1858.

RAPER'S HOTEL, CARDIFF.
Established 1858.

PROPRIETOR:
FREEMAN GRAVIL

69/70 (*Above*) *Raper's Hotel*, on the corner of Westgate Street and Wood Street and adjacent to Wood Street Chapel, had been established for over fifty years when this was taken; (*below*) in 1917 it was bought by the Cardiff & District Congregational Council for use as a centre incorporating a library, Sunday School equipment room, refreshment and appointment rooms, board and committee rooms, and also a hostel 'for young ladies coming strange into the city, pending their obtaining permanent suitable lodgings'

71/72 (*Above*) The *White Swan Inn* on the corner of Bute Street (this section was named Hayes Bridge Road in the mid-1930s) and Bute Terrace. It was closed in 1909. (*Below*) Over half a century later Halewood's shoe shop occupied the same corner site. Now the area has been completely demolished

73 Brain's *Neptune Inn* in Caroline Street was a popular recruiting centre in the First World War

74 Cardiff licensed victuallers' outing to Brecon, 13 October 1921

75 Freeman's cigar factory (then in Grangetown) annual outing to Barry Island, 1929

76 *Tavistock Hotel*, Bedford Street, Roath, regulars on the day of their annual outing, 1925

77 A feature of the *Cow and Snuffers*, Llandaff North, is this sculptured head of Disraeli who is said to have stayed there, although this is unrecorded

78 *Plymouth Arms*, St Fagans, 1908. The name is derived from the Plymouth family

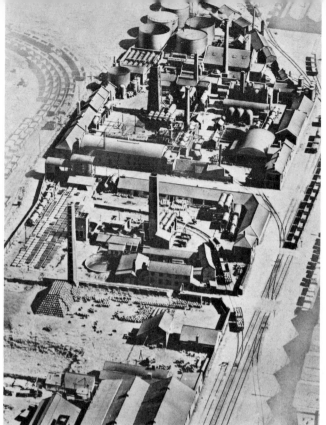

Where MONITOR MOTOR OILS are made by

BIRD & SON Limited

EAST MOORS ROAD, CARDIFF.

80 The annual visit of the Lord Mayor of Cardiff (Alderman Frederick Jones) to the Cardiff Coal and Shipping Exchange, 1943

81 *SS Portugalete*, latest addition to the famous Morel shipping fleet, prepares for her maiden voyage, *c.*1900. The donor's father, Captain Louis Langlois, is on the extreme left

82 Captain Louis Langlois (*centre*) with his first and second officers and chief, second and third engineers, *c.*1900

83 In the early 1900s there were three patent fuel works—Star, Crown and Anchor—on the Glamorganshire Canal between Blackweir and Maindy. Manager of the last named was George Henry Tyler (*left*) who was succeeded by his son Thomas William Tyler. Note the trade mark on the block

84 The blocks were conveyed down the chutes into the waiting boats

85 Inside the Anchor Works trucks discharge their loads to be made into fuel blocks

86 A waiting ship in Bute Docks is being loaded with fuel blocks for France, principal customer
for this trade which ended in 1927

87 King George VI and Queen Elizabeth visited Tremorfa estate on 14 November 1945 to inspect some of the houses built with the help of youngsters employed on a Government sponsored master apprentice scheme run by Cardiff Corporation

88 Some of the Cardiff tradesmen with Huxley Turner (*seated, centre*), a prominent figure in South Wales building circles, who were involved in the scheme

Sport and Entertainment

89/90 Two rare photographs of 'Peerless Jim' Driscoll who was born in Ellen Street, Newtown, in 1880. He turned professional in 1901, won the first Lonsdale Belt in 1910 and ended his career in 1919 when he fought Charles Ledoux at the National Sporting Club in London

Officially, the highest title he ever won was feather-weight champion of the world, but to all who saw him in action he was the finest exponent of scientific boxing the world has ever seen. He died in February 1925 and 100,000 lined the streets of Cardiff to watch the funeral

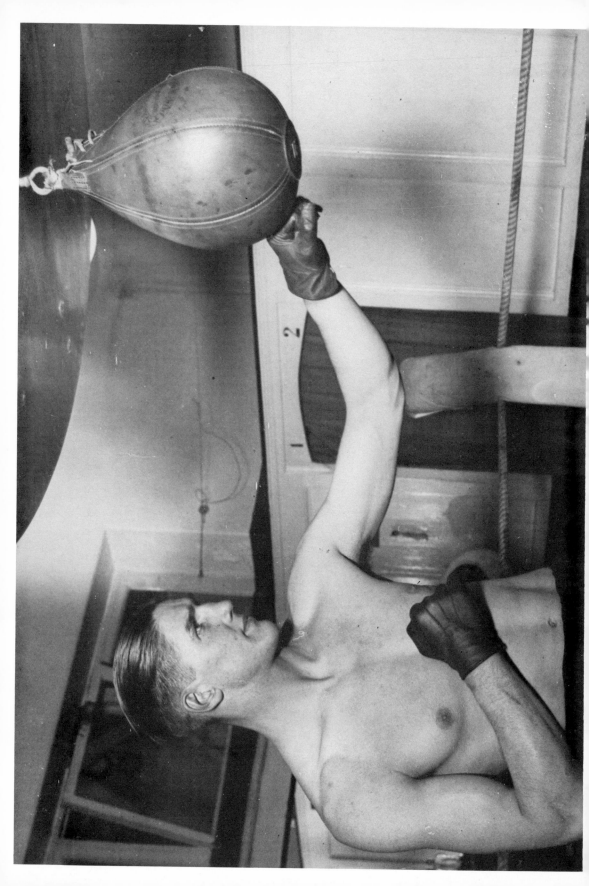

91/92/93 Boxing 'giant' of the 1930s Jack Peterson, after a distinguished career as an amateur, made his professional debut in September 1931 beating Bill Partridge of Poplar in four rounds. He became a household name in July 1932 when he won the British heavy-weight championship and Lonsdale Belt beating Reggie Meen. Until 1937 his stylish brand of boxing drew crowds to Greyfriars Hall, Ninian Park, and leading London venues including the Albert Hall, Wembley, White City and Olympia. He fought, among others, George Cook, Ben Foord, Larry Gains, Jack Pettifer, Charlie Smith, Len Harvey and Walter Neusel. It was the last named who denied Jack his crack at a world title, badly injuring the Cardiff man's eye

JACK PETERSON.
AMATEUR
LIGHT HEAVY WEIGHT & HEAVY WEIGHT
CHAMPION of WALES. 1931.
AND
LIGHT HEAVY WEIGHT
CHAMPION of ENGLAND. 1931.
PROFESSIONAL
HEAVY WEIGHT CHAMPION of WALES. 1932

94 'Pa' Peterson (*centre*) who managed Jack (*left*) and steered him into the boxing big-time. On the right is Don Shortland

95 Roath Amateur Boxing Club, 1919. Included in this group are Fred Yeates (trainer); Fred Perry (*second left, back row*), Olympic Games representative and All Irish light-weight champion of the World at the Tailtean Games in 1932; Ken Brabyn (*fourth left, seated*) and brother Ron (*sixth left, seated*)

96 Albert Donovan enjoyed a fine reputation as an amateur middle-weight boxer and defeated Jack Peterson and Tommy Farr before they gained fame. His proudest moment came at the Dublin Tailtean Games in 1928 when his skill earned him a special award of a bronze statuette which was presented by Gene Tunney. He turned professional and boxed as a welter-weight for a short period before retiring in 1933. He later worked as a boxing trainer/instructor at Oxford University and in the Army

97 Albert Donovan (*second left*) was one of four Welsh amateur boxers who visited Denmark as members of a British team in 1929. They were accompanied by Colonel Kyffin (*centre*) president of the Welsh ABA

98 Ron Brabyn (Roath Amateur Boxing Club), Welsh ABA Schoolboy Champion, 1921, Welsh Senior ABA feather-weight champion, 1934

99 Four Cardiff boxers—Ron Brabyn, Jack Pottinger, T. Jones and W. Manning—were included in this team of Welsh ABA champions who met a Midland Counties ABA team at Birmingham in 1935

100 Once described as 'one of the best middle-weights ever produced in Wales' Phil Edwards was born on 12 May 1936 and turned pro in 1952. In the space of ten years he had 80 fights, winning 70, drawing 3 and losing 7. Still remembered are his clashes with Terry Downes for the British middle-weight championship, both of which he lost despite magnificent displays of skill and courage. When Phil retired in September 1962 Downes paid him a deserved tribute—'No one I have ever met has shown more guts and strength' he said

101 After National Service stationed at Brecon where he was a physical training instructor in the South Wales Borderers Phil joined the Benny Jacobs camp. With him in the Custom House Gym are Benny (*right*) and Archie Rule

102 One of Phil Edwards' few defeats was in 1957 at the hands of Dick Tiger who beat him on points. Tiger went on to become world champion at two weights

103 Phil Edwards at the weigh-in with Martin Hansen at the *Royal Hotel*, Cardiff, in 1959

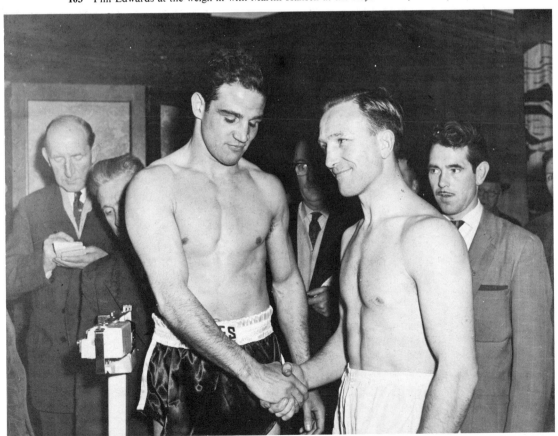

104 Tommy Farr, so nearly the conquering hero after his heavy-weight world title fight against Joe Louis at the Yankee Stadium, New York, in August 1937, seen outside Rumney Pottery where he was presented with a pot in May 1938

105 Staff and management of Guildford Crescent Baths, 1928-30

106 Founded in 1882, Roath Harriers had won many of the Welsh Championships when this was taken in 1931-32

107 Roath Harriers, winners of the *News of the World* Newport—Swansea relay race in the record time of 5 hours, 18 minutes and 20 seconds on 21 November 1936. Captain was E. Hopkins (holding baton). J. W. L. Alford, an outstanding pre-war athlete, is second from the left in the back row

HEATH CRICKET CLUB,
1910.

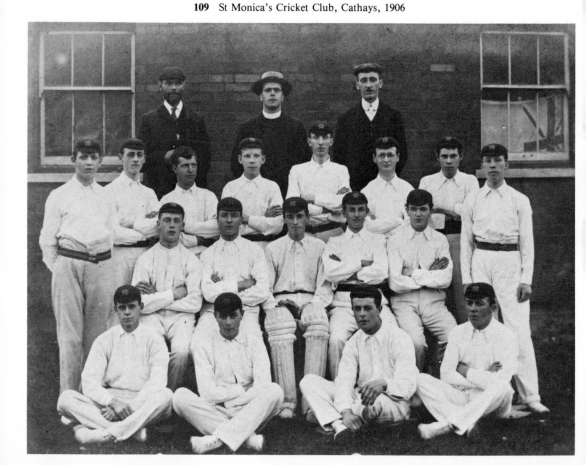

A. BLACKMORE   E. LLEWELLYN.   W. JOHNSON.   E. EDWARDS.   L. JONES.   W. J. MORRIS.   J. H. WHITE   F. WEBSTER   H. LE VESCONTE.   C. WILLIAMS.   W. H. THURSTON   F. CARDER.
(Secretary).   (Committee).   (Vice-Captain).

F. C. MOON.   J. LAWLER.   W. PULLEN   SGT. MAJOR BRYANT.   SGT. J. H. PHILIP   D. HOUSTON.   W. H. MORRIS.
(Captain),   (Committee).

F. W. THOMAS.   J. H. WHITE   R. THOMAS.
(Scorer).

108   Even the book of rules was on display for this 1910 team picture

109   St Monica's Cricket Club, Cathays, 1906

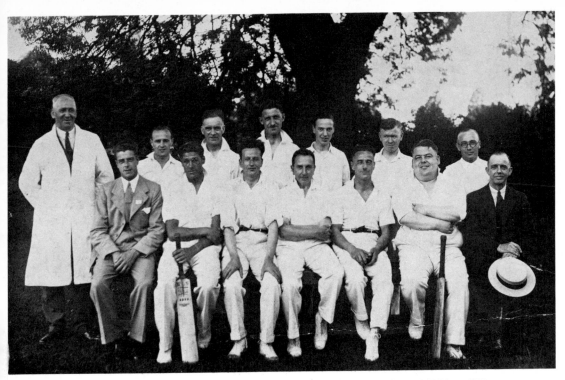

110 Cardiff City Electricity Department (office staff) cricket XI at Llandaff Fields, *c.*1930

111 Stacey Road School cricket team, League Champions 1944. John Tyler, the well-known Cardiff entertainer, is fourth from the right in the third row standing

112 Roath Park Old Boys' baseball team, 1928-29

113 Cardiff Athletic baseball team, 1936, taken in front of the Cricket Pavilion on the Arms Park. Welsh rugby international Ronnie Boon is seated extreme left

114 Curran's baseball team, cup winners 1945. International Freddy Fish is second left, seated

115 Mackintosh FC, 1898-99. S. Candy was captain. Standing second left is Walter Riden, Fred Keenor's schoolmaster who was later at Stacey Road School

116   City Juniors, Roath, soccer team 1907-08

117   St Patrick's School soccer team, 1925-26

B. Lee. J. Flaherty. J. Drennan. J. Gillard. J. Thorne.
B. Broom. T. Doran. H. Rowlands. Mgr. Irvine. (Captain) G. Chorley. J. Mahoney. T. Lyons.

118 Severn Road School soccer team, 1925-26. Albert Bosse (captain)

119 Aubrey Kinnerley was the sports master and B. Pitten the captain of this Adamsdown school team

120   Roath Park soccer team, 1925-26

121   Bob Frank, Herbert Thompson and Cardiff Boys'
rugby cap, 1936-37. Bleddyn Williams was also a
member of this Dewar Shield winning XV. The cup was
presented to Bob for winning the Cardiff Schools' 100
yards sprint in 1937

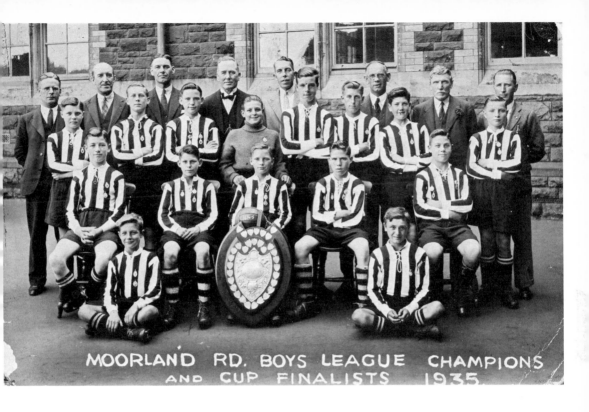

MOORLAND RD. BOYS LEAGUE CHAMPIONS
AND CUP FINALISTS 1935.

122/123 Two outstanding Splott soccer teams—Moorland Road School, 1935 (*above*) and Swansea Street Methodist Mission team, 1938. Cardiff City's Welsh international Billy James, whose promising career was cut short by the Second World War, is in both teams seated second left (*above*) and seated extreme left (*below*)

124 Severn Road School soccer team, cup and shield winners, 1937-38

125 Windsor-Clive School soccer team at Ninian Park for the Seager Cup final in 1939. A. Boulton was captain. Ken Devonshire (*extreme left, back row*) later signed for Cardiff City

126 Cardiff Schools' Football League, 1941-42, winners of the Welsh Schools' Shield. Captain was L. Davies

127 Cardiff Schools' Football League, 1943-44, Welsh Schools' Shield winners. Captain was M. Lloyd

128 Cardiff Schools' Football League, 1944-45. Long serving officials C. Dunn (Secretary) and
R. Loosemore (Chairman) are in the back row. Captain was T. Deans

129 Alan Harrington, later to find fame with Cardiff City, is second from the right in the front
row of this 1946-47 Cardiff Schools' Football League XI. Captain was R. Davenport

130 Herbert Thompson School, Ely, boxing team, 1949

131 Herbert Thompson School rugby team 1950-51

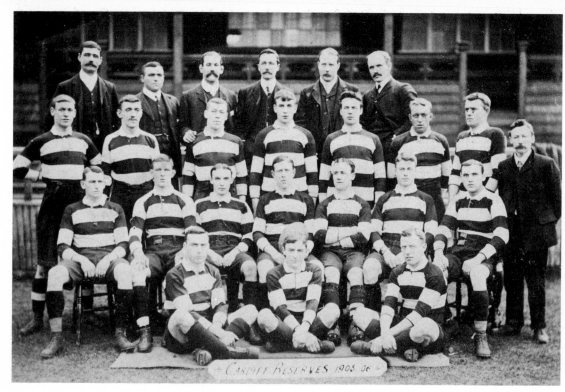

132 Cardiff RFC reserves, 1905-06

133 Splott Crusaders RFC, 1909-10

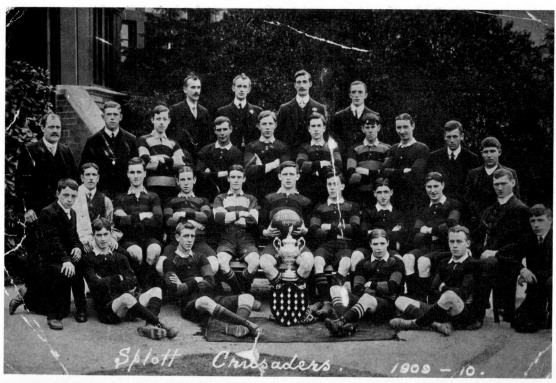

134 The thrill of a lifetime for skipper Fred Keenor as he displays the FA Cup in the Wembley dressing rooms after Cardiff City's historic 1927 cup final win

135 Four years later City were languishing in the Third Division (South). This side lost 2-1 to Coventry on 7 September 1931, Jimmy McCambridge (*centre, front*) scoring the side's goal. He ended the season with 26 goals and City were placed ninth. Also in this team was Walter Robbins (*extreme right, front*)

136 Cardiff City, champions of the Third Division (South), 1946-47. (*Back row, left to right*) Bob Allison (trainer), Billy Baker, Stan Richards, Dan Canning, Glyn Williams, Bernard Ross; (*front row*) Colin Gibson, Billy Rees, Arthur Lever, Fred Stansfield (captain), Alf Sherwood, George Wardle. Outstanding in this perfectly blended side was centre forward Stan 'Open the Score' Richards who netted 30 of City's 93 goals, a club record.

137/138 The name Waldini (Wally Bishop) is synonymous with entertainment in Cardiff. His gypsy band, in their colourful costumes, were a popular attraction in local theatres and at Roath Park Pavilion in the 1930s. During the war Waldini travelled many thousands of miles entertaining the Forces at home and abroad. Vocalists in the band photograph are the Pereira Sisters

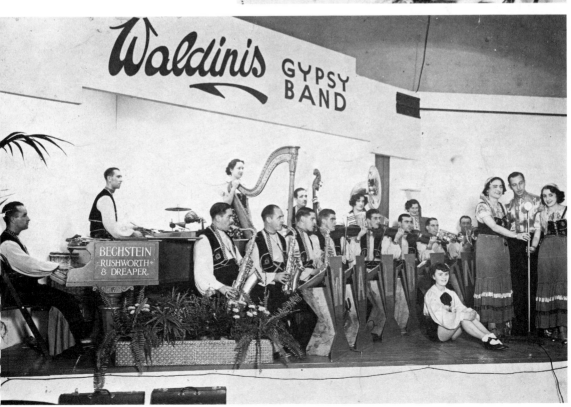

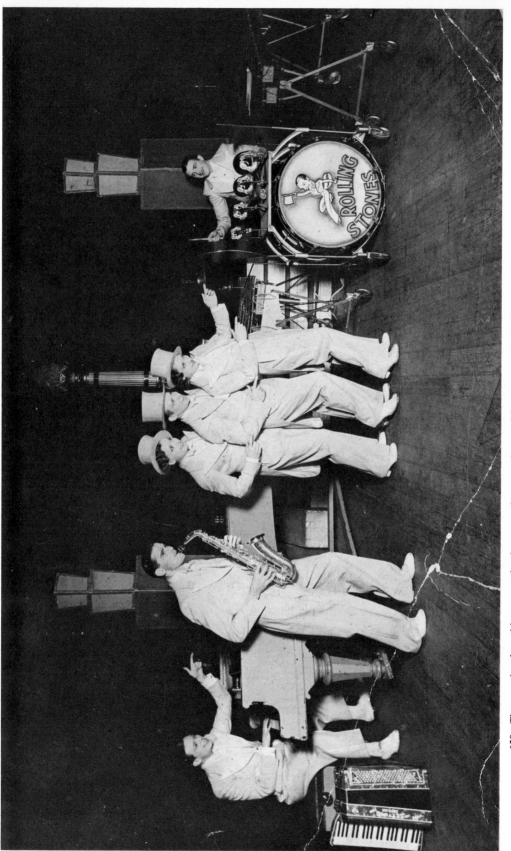

139 They say there's nothing new under the sun, and to prove it, over fifty years ago the 'Rolling Stones' were a popular local show band. The drummer, Ossie Noble, went on to make his name as a speciality act in music hall, while the young alto saxophonist, Reg Hoskins, was just embarking upon a musical career which has since taken him on to the stand with every band of note in the Cardiff area. Reg now lives in retirement at Hollybush, Whitchurch

140/141 Dozens of dance halls throughout the city gave plenty of work to a small army of semi-professional musicians between the wars. A familiar figure was trumpeter Jack Julian seen (*above*) with the New Ambassadors band playing for a tennis dance at Rhiwbina in 1934, and (*below*) with the Astoria Dance Band at Rhiwbina Scouts Hall in 1937

142 Outside the Railway Institute, Newport Road, before playing for a Saturday night gig in 1940 (*left to right*) Bert Miller, Jack Julian, George Marriott, Wally Bright and Ron Lanchberry

143 Shooting a scene for the film 'Tiger Bay' in 1958. The location was Loudoun Square and the extras, seen grouped in front of Horst Buchholz (*centre*) and in the distance, were locals. Behind the camera is the director, J. Lee Thompson

Religion, Education and Public Service

144 St Peter's Church, Roath, *c*.1870-71. Opened in 1861, this photograph shows why in its early days it was known as St Peter-in-the-Fields. St Peter's School was built to the left of the porch in 1872, the Presbytery in April 1873 and the tower was completed at the expense of Lord Bute in 1883

145 All Saints Church, Tyndall Street, opened in December 1856 as an Anglican Welsh Church. It was closed and sold to the GWR in 1901 who used it successively as a power house, biscuit store and road transport maintenance depot. Now derelict and awaiting demolition

146 Roath Road Wesleyan Chapel, *c*.1872. Extensively war damaged in March 1941 and demolished in 1955. Roath Road was changed to Newport Road *c*.1874 but the chapel retained its original name throughout its life

147 Old Vicarage, St John's Street, demolished in 1873. Part of the nave of St John's Church can be seen on the right. The vicarage removed to 40 Charles Street where it remained until the mid-1930s when the present vicarage was built in Cathedral Road

148 Old St Margaret's Church, Roath, in 1865. The new church was consecrated in July 1870 and contains a mausoleum in which the First Marquess of Bute and members of his family are interred

149   St Augustine's Church, Rumney, 1908

150   The Roman Catholic Archbishop of Cardiff, the Rev. Francis Mostyn, blessing and laying the foundation stone of St Patrick's Church, Grangetown, on St Patrick's Day 1929

151 Rev. Hughes was still minister at Ebenezer in 1932. The church in Ebenezer Street was demolished in February 1978 and all trace of its location disappeared with the building of Cardiff's new St David's Shopping Centre

152 Monkton House School, 18 The Parade, 1918

153 Miss Vaughan's ladies' boarding school *c*.1875, now the site of Adamsdown Square. Formerly in Crockherbtown, it moved to Adamsdown House in the mid-1850s probably after the death of its previous owner, Whitlock Nicholl, of the eminent Vale of Glamorgan family

154 St Illtyd's College, Form II A, 1930-31

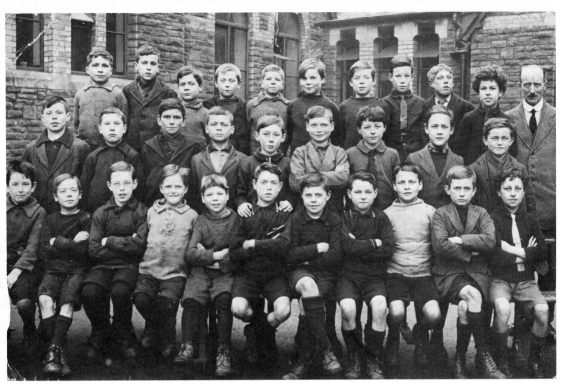

155 Tredegarville Boys' School, Standard II, 1921-22

156 Clarence Road Boys' School, 1928

157 Grange Council School, 1932. Three of these lads achieved sporting fame—Cardiff City and Wales centre forward Stan Richards (*fifth left, second row from front*), international baseballer Fred Hayes (*fourth left, third row*) and boxer Leo Keeley (*seventh left, fourth row*)

158 Catholic Scout Guild's patrol leaders' course outside St Peter's Hall in Northcote Lane, 1934

159/160 4th Cardiff (St Andrews) Scout Troop, *c.*1912, in the backyard of the parish hall in Wyeverne Road. Still in existence after 74 years, it is one of the oldest in the principality

161   6th Cardiff Troop, Boy Scouts, trek cart crew in Roath Park, *c*.1913

162   Boys' Brigade at drill in Cathays Park, *c*.1890

163/164 Boys' Brigade, 3rd Cardiff Company (Cowbridge Road) in 1912; (*below*) the fife and drum band. Taken outside New Trinity Congregational Church in Theobald Road

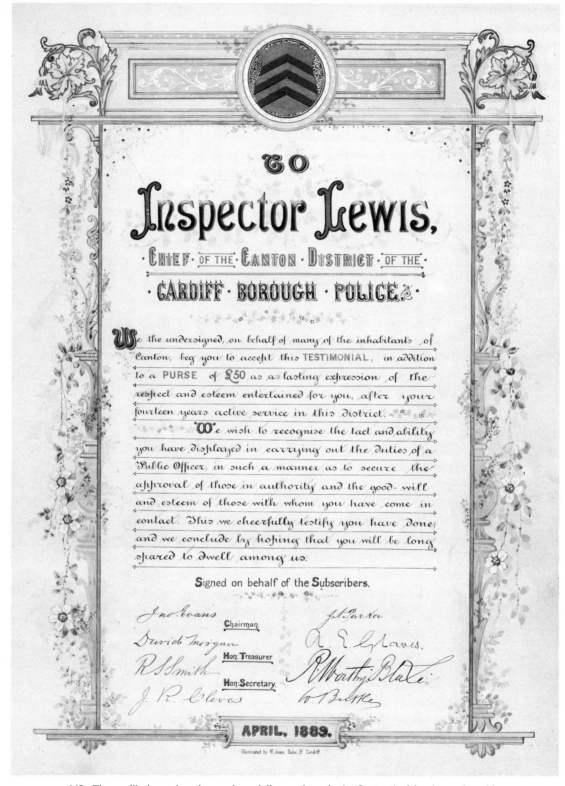

TO

Inspector Lewis,

CHIEF · OF · THE · CANTON · DISTRICT · OF · THE ·
CARDIFF · BOROUGH · POLICE.

We the undersigned, on behalf of many of the inhabitants of Canton, beg you to accept this TESTIMONIAL, in addition to a PURSE of £50 as a lasting expression of the respect and esteem entertained for you, after your fourteen years active service in this district.

We wish to recognise the tact and ability you have displayed in carrying out the duties of a Public Officer, in such a manner as to secure the approval of those in authority and the good-will and esteem of those with whom you have come in contact. This we cheerfully testify you have done; and we conclude by hoping that you will be long spared to dwell among us.

Signed on behalf of the Subscribers.

Jno Evans
Chairman

David Morgan
Hon: Treasurer

R S Smith
Hon: Secretary

J R Clews

J Parker

A E Graves.

R Worthy Blake

W T Burke

APRIL, 1889.

Illuminated by W. Jones, Duke St. Cardiff.

165 There will always be crime and vandalism and no doubt Canton had its share when this public subscription and testimonial was organised for Inspector G. J. Lewis in 1889. In those days, however, law and order, respect and discipline, were generally recognised and often rewarded

166 Probably to mark the occasion of his presentation (No. 165) Inspector G. J. Lewis lined up with his men outside Canton Police Station in 1889. He retired in October 1891 after 29 years' service and died in 1900

167 A Police escort in Bute Street during the Cardiff Seamen's Strike in 1911. The strike, over low wages, Chinese and other foreign 'blackleg' labour, was declared on 14 June and settled on 28 July

168 Isaac Tooze, the first police sergeant of Splott Ward, in his official regalia, *c*.1900. He was
later promoted to Acting Inspector of Roath 'C' Division

169 The Glamorganshire and Monmouthshire Infirmary in Newport Road, *c*.1874. It was built in 1837 and extended in 1866. When the Infirmary was moved to its present site in 1883 this building became the first home of the newly-established University College. It was demolished in 1962

170 The Thomas Andrews Ward in Cardiff Royal Infirmary, 1909

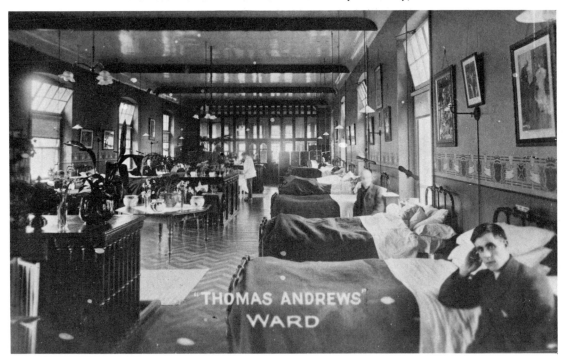

171/172 The present Royal Infirmary was designed by architects James, Seward and Thomas.
(*Above*) Llanbradach Ward during the First World War; (*below*) Shand Children's Ward in 1909

173 Whitchurch Mental Hospital was opened in 1908 with initial accommodation for 750 patients

174 Aga cookers had just been installed in Cardiff Royal Infirmary kitchens when this publicity picture was taken in 1937

Transport

175 Introduced in 1942 with the object of replacing the tramway system, the trolleybus offered the 'lowest fares in Great Britain' and for a time its future looked assured. But rising costs and its dependence upon overhead wires which prevented any appreciable extension beyond the limits of the tramway system brought it into disfavour. By 1970 the last trolleybus had operated and the system was replaced by motorbuses

176 Trolleybus 222 crossing Clarence Bridge on a special enthusiasts' tour on 20 March 1966 to mark the closure of Service 6 Clarence Road and Llandaff Fields (via Wood Street) and Service 9 Gabalfa and Pier Head (via St Mary Street and Wood Street) due to the weight restriction (13 tons) imposed on Wood Street bridge

177/178 Single-deck and double-deck trolleybuses operating on Services 9 and 16 at the Pier Head terminus in 1952

179 Trolleybus 237, bought from Pontypridd UDC, standing at the original Canal Bridge terminus of the Bute Street route. Note the wartime grey livery

180 Trolleybuses at the junction of Neville Street and Lower Cathedral Road in the early 1960s

181 Tramcar and motorbus at the junction of Hayes Bridge Road and Mill Lane in April 1938

182 Tramcar 70 at Clarence Road terminus on the Cathedral Road—Clarence Road service in September 1937

183 Tramcar crossing the original Wood Street bridge and heading in the direction of Grangetown and ultimately the Docks, August 1939

184 On the reverse journey to town a tramcar travels along Tudor Street which has hardly changed after 43 years

185 A tramcar on the Pier Head to Roath Park service seen in Hayes Bridge Road, 1939

186 A couple of open-top tramcars in Lower Bute Street shortly before the First World War

187/188 Victoria Park, terminus for the trams and departure point for 'bus services to Ely estate and Culverhouse Cross. The photographs were taken in August 1940 (*above*) and 1936 when a journey on an open-topper was something special

189 Cardiff Central Station can be seen in the background as single-deck and open-top tramcars discharge their passengers at the southern end of St Mary Street in 1908

190 Llanishen Railway Station, *c*.1910. The Rhymney Railway train would be taking passengers to the terminus at The Parade adjacent to Queen Street

191 Platelayers and staff of Cardiff Railway Company outside Whitchurch Signal Box, September 1918

192 ASLEF Improvement Class, Canton Loco Sheds, 1925. The express locomotive in the background is 4-6-0 Saint Class 2942 'Fawley Court', built in May 1912 and withdrawn December 1949

193 In 1900 railway employment was something to be proud of and when your name was displayed on the side of a guards van job satisfaction was really yours. Richard Jones of Harriet Street, Cathays, in the centre holding the lamp and shunting pole, worked for the Taff Vale Railway for 47 years, six of them as foreman at the Crockherbtown (Cathays) Yard

194 In old age Richard Jones was still proud to wear his TVR hat

195 J. & R. Griffiths' and Sandridge & Company's sand wharves adjoining Harrowby Street on the Glamorganshire Canal, April 1943

196 The Glamorganshire Canal Railway served wharves and warehouses on the west side of the canal between West Canal Wharf and the Sea Lock. This battery-electric shunter was purchased in 1947 by Cardiff Corporation replacing the steam locomotive *Delwyn*. It was sold in 1963 when the railway closed

Memorable Events

197/198 High Street, looking north and south, decorated for the wedding of the Third Marquess of Bute to Gwendolen Mary Anne, daughter of Lord Edward George Fitzalan Howard of Glossop, in May 1872. The bride's family names were given to streets off Newport Road which were being developed at that time

199/200 Incredibly this was a *temporary* building comprising a ballroom, banqueting hall and reception rooms specially built in the Castle forecourt for Lord Bute's coming-of-age banquet and ball on Thursday 10 September 1868. The present banqueting hall above the library was constructed *c*.1873 by dividing the medieval great hall horizontally

201 The *Borough Arms* and Old Market decorated for the wedding of the Marquess of Bute in 1872. The market entrance was demolished to make way for Solomon Andrews' first Market Buildings *c.*1884

202 Queen Mary's last visit to South Wales was on 6 April 1938 when she attended a charity matinée variety concert at the Capitol in aid of two local nursing bodies. Highspot of the show was the Treorchy Male Voice Choir who came straight from their pit shifts in working clothes with their lamps and coal-begrimed faces

203 A scene outside the Ministry of National Service recruiting office on the corner of Bute Terrace and Mary Ann Street in March 1918. The shortage of recruits compelled the Government to call up 'reserved' men from the mines and as a result recruiting offices in the valleys were swamped. This queue was waiting to be medically examined

204 Some of Curran's employees who helped the war effort in 1914-1918

205 Dowlais steelworkers holding a meeting at St Francis' schoolroom, Pontypridd Street (at the junction with Neath Street), Splott, during the 1911 strike

206 These children standing outside Splott Labour Hall in Neath Street with jugs ready for soup typify 'the hungry thirties'

207/208 Albany Road School was used as a Military Hospital during the First World War. Staff and local volunteers helped the boys to make the most of Christmas 1916

209 Ely Civil Defence workers (with mascot) during the Second World War

210 Ely Ward Recreation Committee pose with the 1946 'Holidays at Home' Queen. Councillor T. E. Sweet (*extreme left*) was chairman, and C. H. Flowers (*extreme right*) secretary

211 Coronation celebrations in Milton Street, Roath, 1937

212 'VE' party held in Union Street, May 1945

213 Coronation party in 1937 taken on the corner of Treorchy Street and Merthyr Street, Cathays. The accordionists were Kenny Sheehy and Grace Evans

214 'VE' party in Arabella Street, Roath, May 1945

215 Ely British Legion outside the Law Courts where they attended an annual Gallipoli March in the 1930s. In the front are the Grange Pipers Band with Rev. Redvers C. Evans, Vicar of St David's, Ely

216 Canvassers for Sir Ernest Bennett, the National Government candidate, outside their Whitchurch Road committee rooms during the Parliamentary Election of 1935